KNOWING GOD

Part One

DANIEL BARDEN

For Rosie, Lucy and Noah. May God bless you immensely as you discover the riches of his grace in Christ.

Knowing God

CONTENTS

INTRODUCTION

Theology's fallen on hard times. For most, theology is abstract and should be left in the realm of ideas. It's fine for book-nerds and pastors, but it doesn't have much relevance in day-to-day life. I remember once being in a conversation with a young man. We were discussing men's groups and I urged the person to consider something theological, perhaps the doctrine of salvation. I was thrilled with the prospect and thought that this would really benefit the men in the congregation. But I was met with a puzzled look and a response that went something like, "that doesn't sound very relevant. We should shoot for something more grounded in every-day life." I was taken aback and couldn't believe the response. How could the knowledge of God appear irrelevant to anyone? My hunch is that the pushback isn't novel to this individual. There's a growing trend in evangelical circles that theologising is fruitless. Why waste endless hours considering doctrine when we could be equipping the saints in their work, parenting and evangelistic endeavours? Why muse God's simplicity when we could help church members in their growth in holiness? We have far too many problems in the church to be concerned with crossing our theological t's, don't we?

Why this matters

I understand the concern. But let me begin with the words of John Webster who said that theology is the knowledge of God and all things in relation to God. This simple yet profound sentence reveals that theology isn't the stuff of ivory towers. Theology is for God's people who need to grow in their relationship with God. To parrot the words of John Calvin, "all true knowledge consists in the knowledge of God and the knowledge of self."[1] In other words, there's nothing more important for people like us than to grow and deepen in our understanding of who God is. Think for a moment of the words of Christ in his high priestly prayer. Jesus said that eternal life is to know God and to know his Son (John 17:3). It's a profound statement, but Jesus isn't saying anything new. God's Old Testament people were destroyed for a lack of knowledge (Hosea 4:6). And so what they needed was a day when the earth would be filled with the *knowledge* of the glory of God (Habakkuk 2:14). To know God is to experience life. Jesus isn't talking about knowledge in some pantheistic sense. This is knowledge of the only true God, the God who has revealed himself in Christ. Since salvation comes by grace alone through faith alone in Christ alone, we need to know who God

---

[1] John Calvin, *Institutes of the Christian Religion,* ed. John T. McNeil, trans. Ford Lewis Battles, Library of Christian Classics (Philadelphia: Westminster, 1960), 1.1.1

is.   We can't believe in the God we don't know. And so in one sense we can say that to meditate on God is an end in itself. The Westminster Catechism could have said that *the chief end of man is to glorify God and consider him forever.*

The fountain

A. W. Tozer once said that what we believe about God is the most important thing about us. Read that again and let the words wash over you. What is the most important thing about me? It's not the work I do, the family I have, the money in my wallet, my status in society, or the friends I make. We are pretty good at making good things, ultimate things. But none of these things are central. The most important thing about me is what I believe about God. Why is that? Because what I believe about God then flows into everything else I believe and practise. In other words, the knowledge of God is the fountain, and everything else is the stream. Let me give one example. Our view of salvation is hooked and dependent on what we believe about God. If God is sovereign and in complete control, then salvation is fully and finally of the LORD. If God is not sovereign and not in complete control, then salvation is in part the achievement of man because God is unable to move until humans exercise their free will. What we believe about God flows into everything else we believe. And so this matters more than we might think. Theology is the knowledge of God and all things in relation to God. Theology is to contemplate, consider and know the God who has rescued us in Christ. To do theology is to deepen and grow in our knowledge and love of our Triune God. To abandon theology is to be stifled, ignorant and distant.

Head and heart

This book is designed to help each of us come to know and love the God who has revealed himself in the world, his word and his Son. At times it will be stretching. Some things may go over our heads. That's not a surprise because the God we're considering together is infinite in glory and majesty. It would be more worrying if we could contain and box up the God who dwells in eternity. But I also hope we leave stunned, breathless and amazed. I don't want us to close the final page thinking, "Great! Now I've finally sorted God out in my head." I want us leaving thinking, "Wow! This God is amazing! I want to get down and worship him." If at any point you're left in awe, then the work has achieved its aim.

Mapping the doctrine of God

The layout of the book is simple enough. But the decision was not easy. There's a decision to make whether to begin with God's Oneness or his Threeness; to begin with the attributes of God or the Three distinct Person's of the Trinity. There are pros and cons with starting in both places. But we need to start somewhere. And so I have gone with the Western tradition which means we will begin with the attributes of God and eventually move to the Three Peron's of the Godhead. It's not a simple divide because we can't consider the One without being drawn to the Three. As Gregory of Nazianzus famously mused,

No sooner do I conceive of the One than I am illumined by the Splendour of the Three; no sooner do I distinguish Them than I am carried back to the One. When I think of any One of the Three I think of Him as the Whole, and my eyes are filled, and the greater part of what I am thinking of escapes me. I cannot grasp the greatness of That One so as to attribute a greater greatness to the Rest. When I contemplate the Three together, I see but one torch, and cannot divide or measure out the Undivided Light.[2]

---

[2] Gregory of Nazianzus, *Oration 40: One Holy Baptism*, in *Nicene and Post-Nicene Fathers*, 2nd series, ed. Philip Schaff and Henry Wace (New York: Christian Literature, 1893), 7:375.

1

INCOMPREHENSIBLE

When we encounter something spectacular, we find it both humbling and fascinating. We are hard-wired for God and so there's an unquenchable itch that doesn't go away. We're moved by snow-capped mountains, gushing waterfalls and the deep blue of the ocean. We have an unquenchable thirst for glory. King David looked up at the starry night sky and declared "The heavens declare the glory of God" (Psalm 19:1). I remember stepping foot in Rome's Pantheon. As I slowly edged closer to the entrance and walked through those towering doors my breath was taken away and I was dwarfed by its beauty. All of these moments point us to the Ultimate Beautiful One behind it all.

God is incomprehensible

I want us to begin our study with a dilemma. We are made by God and for God. And yet the God we're designed for is incomprehensible to the human mind. I know that seems like a contradiction. You're probably re-reading the title of the book and now wondering why we're beginning with the fact that we can't know God (hold that thought)! That God is incomprehensible has been the consistent teaching of the church. This is what the Second London Baptist Confession says in Article 2, Paragraph 1,

> The Lord our God is one, the only living and true God. He is self-existent and infinite in being and perfection. His essence *cannot be understood* by anyone but himself. He is unchangeable, immense, eternal, *incomprehensible,* almighty.

In other words, God is radically different from the creation that he has made. To affirm that God is incomprehensible is to say that God is God. It's also to admit that there is a vast distinction between the Creator and the creature. Think of the watery chasm between Britain and the United States. And then multiply that gap by infinity! The difference between God and creation isn't just quantitative, as though God is a bigger, better version of his creation. The difference is qualitative, he's in a different category altogether. It's easy for us to limit God in human terms. Think with me for a moment about Usain Bolt. He'd wipe the floor with all of us in a 100m sprint. To enter is to lose. Every facet of Usain's body is more enhanced to run the race. He's quantitatively better than us. But God isn't like that. He isn't in the same race, only a few steps ahead. He's on a different playing field. This is what fallen humanity finds so hard to receive and accept. The history of the human race is one long attempt to climb the ladders of mysticism and moral effort. We do everything we can to climb to God and manipulate him. But the Bible tells us that the vision of God in his naked glory is deadly to us. Recall the conversation that Moses had with God in the book of Exodus. Moses asked to see God's face. And God said, "No one can see my face and live". (Exodus 33:20). In 1 Timothy 6:15 Paul says that the immortal, invisible and eternal God dwells in unapproachable light. No one has known the mind of the Lord (Romans 11:34), and God's thoughts are higher than our own (Isaiah 55:8-9).

To comprehend God is to be God

And so do you get the picture? God isn't this puzzle for us to try and figure out. He is the Almighty Creator who wraps himself in light. God's in a different category to us and that's meant to leave us in awe and wonder. Before you close the book in despair, I want to help us see that this is a good thing. Just consider what it would mean it we were able to grasp all that God is. It would mean that we would be gods. If we could grasp the infinite God, then we'd have the infinite mind of God. Augustine said, "We are speaking of God. Is it any wonder you don't comprehend?"[3] Aquinas also said, "The infinite cannot be contained in the finite. God exists infinitely and nothing can grasp him infinitely. It's impossible for a created mind to understand God infinitely; therefore, it is impossible to comprehend him."[4] Here are a couple of imperfect illustrations... It would be like my one-year-old daughter trying to comprehend me. It's impossible for her little mind. She cannot grasp the complexity that makes me, me. She doesn't know my past experiences. She doesn't know the places I've visited, the sights I've seen, the music I've heard and the food I've tasted. My daughter

---

[3] Augustine, *Lectures on the Gospel of John,* tractate 38; as quoted in Bavinck, *Reformed Dogmatics,* 2:48.
[4] Aquinas, *Summa Theologiae* 1a.12.7.

can't comprehend me, and that's a creature-creature distinction! Imagine the gap that exists between God and his creatures! Or to flip the analogy, comprehending God is like trying to take in the details of the entire cosmos with a single telescope. It's never going to happen. But even here the analogy breaks down because the cosmos has an end, God doesn't.

And so what does all of this mean? It means that at the end of our passionate desire to climb the ladder to God, we find a Being of blinding glory, pure holiness, dreadful justice, and a love that destroys the unlovely. Any attempt at seeking to climb into the presence of God is like a dry branch within a holy fire. We must begin by grasping the fact that God is dangerous, other, and dwells in unapproachable light. John tells us that no one has ever seen God (John 1:18). This is where true theology begins. God is God and we are not. This fundamental truth strikes at the heart of human pride and arrogance. Ever since the garden, humanity has wanted to claim the Divine throne. Adam and Eve weren't content on being made in the image of God. They wanted to be God. But here's where the rubber hits the road... God is in a different category to us. He can't be comprehended by finite creatures. God is God and we are not.

The great descent

Now at this point you might be wondering, "why bother?" Shouldn't we just throw our hands in the air and give up? Shouldn't we conclude with the mystics and agnostics that we cannot know God? Perhaps they have it right? God is the great unknown. Well, here's the good news. Yes, the scriptures testify that God can't be comprehended by his creatures. But it also testifies that God by his own free decision decided to stoop down to our level and reveal himself to us. We can't climb the ladder to God through our own mystical pursuits. But God in his grace has descended to us. We can't bridge the chasm, but God has. As incomprehensible as it might seem, God has made us for the purpose of knowing him. And God reveals himself by speaking human words. Theologians call this *accommodation*. God has accommodated himself to us with words that we can understand. John Calvin calls it baby speech. Just as a baby can't understand its parents without baby talk, so we can't understand God without creaturely words.

Think about how scripture speaks of God's omniscience. Proverbs 15:3 says, the eyes of the Lord are everywhere, keeping watch on the wicked and the good. We both know that God doesn't literally have eyes because he's spirit, not body (John 4:24). Movies and picture books don't help us out, and so please don't picture an old grey-bearded Santa Claus sitting in the clouds with eyes, arms, legs and a body. God doesn't have a body because he is spirit. And so what's going on in Proverbs 15? By attributing eyes to God, the scriptures are conveying to us that God knows all things. We might think that our thoughts and actions are hidden from God, but

God sees all that we do. The wicked won't get away with their wickedness. And those clothed in the righteousness of Christ will be watched over by a God who cares and loves them.

General Revelation

And so God uses human words to convey truth about himself. Without these words, we cannot grasp anything of who God is. Even the creation is a form of God's speech. "The heavens declare the glory of God and the sky above proclaim his handiwork. Day to day pours out speech, night to night reveals knowledge" (Psalm 19:1-2). When we take a stroll outside and look up at the stars, we're gazing at a stunning canvas. And this canvas is preaching to us. It's preaching that a powerful, loving Creator has hand-fashioned the universe. Romans 1 tells us that because of this general revelation, man is without excuse. Not one person will be able to claim ignorance on the day of judgement. God has made it abundantly clear that he exists. In simple terms, a building assumes a builder and a painting assumes a painter. The world points to the Creator, and through this world God has made himself known.

Special Revelation

But this isn't enough. If humanity was left with creation alone, it would be guess work. We would know that *a* god exists. We might guess that this god is powerful, wise, just and good. But we wouldn't know what his character is like towards us. That's why there are millions of gods in the world today. Different religions have tried to guess what God is like from creation. Maybe God is like an elephant, or an eagle, or a cat, or a person. Creation doesn't give us the kind of knowledge that we need to have a relationship with God. Which is why Psalm 19 goes on to say in verse 7 that "the law of the LORD is perfect, reviving the soul; the testimony of the LORD is sure, making wise the simple". What we all need is for God to speak to us in the scriptures. Theologians call this *special revelation.* The Bible corrects our distortion of general revelation. When we take a night stroll and imagine God by looking at the stars, we can only guess. But with scripture, the fog disappears. We have a God who comes down to our level and speaks simple words we can all understand. Someone once said that the book of creation declares the glory of the Creator. The book of salvation declares the glory of the Redeemer. With the Bible we can enter a relationship with the God who longs to be known. It's the equivalent of putting on a pair of glasses for the first time. The haze is gone.

With that being said I want us to avoid something. We don't want to reduce God down to the level of his own words in the Bible. The Bible still speaks of God in a way that protects the gulf that exists between Creator and creature. When we read that God has arms, wings, feet and hands we know that God is using metaphor. The Bible conveys truth analogically. That is, God is similar to the words, but not identical to them. God can be compared with hands and eyes, but not in a literal sense. This means that God speaks to us with anthropomorphic language. Because we are humans with limited minds, God needs to bridge the chasm by bringing human words to us. God describes himself in many ways to enable a relationship to work.

The final way that God has revealed himself to us is in the birth, life, death and resurrection of Jesus Christ. Jesus is the one who makes the invisible God known (John 1:18). He is the image of the invisible God (Colossians 1:15). There is no way to access God in a saving way outside of Jesus Christ. In our sinful condition we need more than just a clearer vision of God's general revelation. We need a word of rescue and a proclamation of forgiveness. We need an alien word about what God has done to justify, redeem and deliver us from our treason. Humanity doesn't stand in a neutral place. We stand condemned because we have broken God's law and rejected his ways. We are rebels in desperate need of grace. And so God delivers the message of his rescue in the person of his Son. God spoke this word to Adam and Eve in the garden when he promised the serpent-crusher (Genesis 3:15). This promise is thread through the rest of the Old Testament and finally culminates when God takes on flesh. The heart of special revelation is that God has justified us in Christ. God has come to rescue sinners in the person of his Son. This is where speculation and mysticism are useless. It doesn't matter what we imagine reality is like, nor whether we believe in one hundred gods or none. Something has happened in history and it can't be wished away. There's an empty tomb in Israel. Those who argue that God can't be known ignore the beating heart of the gospel; that God became flesh in order to live the perfect life we should have lived, and die the death we deserved to die. That's the truth that faith grasps. And so faith involves knowledge. We need to know, not just that God is the Mighty Creator, but that he is a Redeemer for me.

Knowing God

So can we comprehend God in his fullness? No chance because that would make us God! Only the infinite can comprehend the infinite. We can't know God fully. But we can know God truly. That's because God has come down to our level. He's revealed himself to his creation. All of creation sings his praise. And he's made himself known in the scriptures. The bible describes God in lots of ways. He is our rock, a fortress, a husband, shepherd, father, friend and lion. We know instinctively that God isn't literally these things. He's a rock because he's reliable and unchanging. He's a fortress because he's our hiding place in the fiercest of storms. He's a husband who remains faithful to us. He's a shepherd that leads and guides. He's a father that wraps his arms around us. He's a friend who sticks close. He's a lion who triumphs on our behalf. Above all, he is the God and Father of the Lord Jesus Christ who pursues the runaway, draws near to the broken-hearted and rescues the rebel. It's fruitless to try and find God through mysticism. To know God we need to look in the face of Jesus.

2

A SE

I have a hunch that most of us have wondered what God was doing before he made the world. This conundrum was something that really caused my brain to tick. I used to sit down and wonder, "*What* was God doing before he made the cosmos? *Where* was he? *When* was he? Do these questions even make sense?" At first, I perhaps imagined that God was bored. He was hovering around twiddling his thumbs. And then a lightbulb came on. God had a brilliant idea. He thought to himself, "I know what I'll do. I'll make a universe and plant little image bearers on a sphere called earth so that I'm not lonely anymore!" So eventually God made people, and when God did that, he felt immensely full and satisfied. Before creation God was bored. Now that we're on the scene, everything's so much better!

Perhaps that's how you view things. But here's the thing... God wasn't bored, and he wasn't lacking fulness. That would be true of a human-like idol. It might be true of Odin and Thor. But it's not true of the one, true and everlasting God. Here is truth that might sting a bit... God doesn't need you and he doesn't need me. By grace he chooses us, loves us and draws near to us. But he doesn't need us as if he has a lack and we meet that need. It's not like God was bored and lonely, and he needed us to fill a void in his heart. God creates out of sheer generosity and love. We gain from creation, but God doesn't. And the reason for that is because God is self-existent and independent. God is reliant on no one. He has Life in himself.

This is one of the big distinctions between God the Creator and his creatures. You and I are reliant on every breath we take. The scriptures say that in God we live and move and have our being (Acts 17:28). God gives life and breath to us, but he exists in himself. He doesn't need anything to be who he is. He doesn't need temples to dwell in, money to store, or followers on Facebook. God's life is his own, ours is borrowed. God has existed in perfect and eternal happiness as Father, Son and Spirit. That's what God was doing before creation. He was fully and totally happy in himself. The Father loved and cherished his Son. The Son eternally imaged the glory of his Father. The Spirit is the eternal love that binds them together. God was blessed, happy and satisfied.

God is self-existent

Self-existence is what we mean when we say that God is *a se*. God's aseity is one of the first things we find in the 1689 London Baptist Confession of faith. Chapter 2, Paragraph 1 says,

> The Lord our God is one, the only living and true God. He is *self-existent*.

What does this mean? It means that God exists in himself. He isn't dependent on anything or anyone to be who he is. He's the uncaused cause. Have a listen to these words from Herman Bavinck,

> God is absolute being, the fullness of being, and therefore also eternally and absolutely independent in his existence, perfections, in all his works, from first to last, the sole cause and final goal of all things.[5]

26

All of that is to say that God's life differs from our own. God's life is infinite and has no start or end date. The good news for us is that it means that God can supply every need because he remains perfectly satisfied in himself. God's self-sufficiency reminds us that every need we have will be supplied by the God who is perfect, in need of nothing.

The Divine Name

But at this point you may be wondering what the Bible has to say about all of this! Have we entered the realm of metaphysics and mysticism and left God's spoken word behind? This is where Exodus 3:14 becomes important. Exodus 3 is the famous account of the burning bush. Moses finds himself captivated by a burning bush that's not consumed, and so he

---

[5] Herman Bavinck, *Reformed Dogmatics,* vol. 2, *God and Creation,* ed. John Bolt, trans. John Vriend (Grand Rapids, MI: Baker Academic, 2004), 152

goes over to the bush. And to his amazement, Yahweh, the God of his fathers speaks from within. Yahweh initiates a conversation with Moses about his plans to rescue his people and liberate them from Egyptian slavery. It's then that Moses asks the key question, "If I come to the people of Israel and say to them, 'the God of your fathers has sent me to you,' and they ask me, 'What is his name?' what shall I say to them?" It's a fair question. And God's responds with those immortal words in verse 14, "I AM WHO I AM. Say this to the people of Israel, 'I AM has sent me to you... the LORD, the God of your fathers, the God of Abraham, the God of Isaac, and the God of Jacob has sent me to you.'" God's words are so rich and breath-taking that we can hardly do them justice in such a short space. To say that this is one of the most important revelations in the Bible is a massive understatement. The first thing to say is that no translation can summarise it perfectly. If you have an ESV, then you probably have a footnote

which says, "I AM WHAT I AM" or "I WILL BE
WHAT I WILL BE." In truth, any of these would
work. And so, what is God doing? What is God
saying? God is assigning himself the verb – to be.
In other words, to exist. It's as if God is saying, "I
exist that I exist. Existence is identical with my
nature. I am pure existence itself. If you want to
know what I'm like, then you need to consider
the verb 'to be'." This is a God that is radically
other and different to anything else we've ever
seen or known. This isn't a God we can easily
manipulate and box in. It's a God who has always
been and will always be. Furthermore, this is a
God who is being itself. Doesn't that cause the
reflex of awe and wonder? Isn't that spectacular
and eye-popping? This is a God that's worthy of
our praise. No wonder Moses was told to remove
his sandals. This is holy ground indeed.

The God of gods

One thing that is worth considering is that God's revealed name comes in the context of the whole Exodus narrative. God's people are currently chained up in Egypt. They're slaves and surrounded by a pagan culture. This means that they were surrounded by all kinds of Egyptian deities. Perhaps you know some of them. Osiris, Horus, Ptah, and Hathor to name a few. But the common theme with all the gods of Egypt was how human-like they were. And if not human, then animalistic. They were often portrayed with having animal heads and human bodies. This meant that they were glorified humans, and gods in reference to things in creation. They're the kinds of gods that humans would make. They're not impressive or *other*.

The Canaanite gods were like that too. Baal was the god of the storm cloud, but he wasn't the god of fertility. Anat was the god of the underworld, but she wasn't the god of war. Asherah was the god of fertility, but she wasn't the god of harvest. The Canaanite gods were limited, earthy, unimpressive. The same goes for the Greek gods. Athena was the mighty god of war. Aphrodite was the sensual god of love. Zeus was the great god of thunder. There's one thing that strikes you when you read their accounts. They look so much like us. In other words, they're glorified humans. They have affairs. They get frustrated. They deceive each other. They cause wars and schisms. They're big bosses with special powers. All of them are in charge of a particular field in the world. This means they're dependent creatures. They're also dependent on humanity for their own being. It's possible to offend and upset them. If we ignore the ancient gods, they get angry and strike us with missiles. If we serve them and worship, then they grow happy and fond of us. When we take the wrong path, they grow miserable and irritable. Do you see the problem? They're big humans with big superpowers. They're certainly not the great I AM. And so, I hope you can see the difference. I wonder if the Israelites noticed it too. Did they have reason to fear the Egyptian gods? Was there a reason for them to rest in Horus? The answer is an easy no, because Horus is a dependent being (in fact, he doesn't exist at all). But the God of Abraham, Isaac and Jacob is totally *other*. The God of the Bible cannot be contained. The Egyptian gods are much easier to grasp and understand, aren't they? It would be much easier to write an entire book on the gods of Egypt. We can grasp them because they're humans with special powers. They're easy to comprehend. They're not incomprehensible. But the true and living God is nothing like that. To get to the core of Israel's God we need to grasp that he simply *is*. God isn't dependent on anything or anyone. He doesn't need us to make him happy. If you begin to drink this in, you'll be terribly liberated. Sometimes we treat a relationship with God like an episode of Britain's Got Talent. We act as though we're on the stage and we need to try and squeeze an approval out of God. We need to do something impressive to please him and make him happy.

We're worried that we'll perform the wrong way and make him sad. Of course, we can't negate the fact that we're called to please our Father and live for his glory. But we shouldn't for a moment imagine that God is dependent on our actions to be who he is. We'll return to this in a later chapter when we consider the doctrine of God's impassibility. I don't serve God as if he needs anything. It's God who gives me life, breath and everything else (Acts 17:25). And that is breath-taking news for people like us! If God is free and not dependent on me to be who he is, then he is free to give me salvation irrespective if I've performed enough for him.

3

SIMPLE

Now I don't blame you if you're puzzled while reading this chapter heading. God is simple? After all we've been discussing? How can we move from incomprehensibility and aseity to simplicity? Every time I teach God's simplicity, I'm met with confused faces and a conversation that goes something like, "No he's not! God's big and complex. He's not simple! Using a spoon is simple. God isn't simple!" But here's the thing... Simplicity doesn't mean that God is simple to understand. Simplicity means that God is not composed of parts. I would say (almost ironically) that this is one of the most complex aspects of the doctrine of God, and so do your best to stay with me.

And have a listen to the 1689 confession,

God is a perfectly pure spirit. He is invisible and has no body, *parts* or passions.

What is the confession saying? It's saying that God isn't like a pie as if we slice the pie up into different pieces. Sometimes we think of God in this way. God has lots of different attributes. God is ten percent love, fifteen perfect holiness, seven percent merciful, and so on. There are plenty of people who suggest that some attributes in God are bigger and more central than others. The one that usually takes the cake is the attribute of God's love. God's love trumps all other attributes and makes the rest of them disappear like the Cheshire Cat. But this simple can't be. To begin with, the Bible tells us that God *is* his attributes. God doesn't have or possess love, he *is* love (1 John 4:8). God doesn't have light, he *is* light (1 John 1:5). God doesn't have holiness, he *is* holiness (Isaiah 6). This is where the doctrine of God's aseity comes into the picture. And this is why the doctrine of God is like one big Jenga tower. If you remove just one piece, the whole tower crashes down. Because God is not dependent on anything, he is simple. God is not composed of different parts. As a human being I'm composed of different things. I have a soul and a body. I have a mind, limbs and organs. I need all these things to be me. And so notice that I am fully dependent on these things. I'm not a se (like God), I'm a dependent creature. If this is hard to grasp, then picture a Lego man.[6] The Lego man is dependent on two things. He's dependent on all the pieces put together. That is, he can only be himself when he's fully made. Otherwise, he's just a pocketful of pieces. And second, he's dependent on a composer to put him together. Because the Lego man is made of pieces, he needs someone to compose him. Every illustration breaks down, but I hope it helps you grasp something of God's simplicity. It's impossible for God to be composed of different attributes or parts. If he were, then he would be dependent on all the pieces to be who he is. And

---

[6] I heard this first from James Dolezal

he'd be dependent on something bigger to put him together). I hope this helps you to see why this matters and what's at stake. If we lose simplicity, then we lose aseity. And if we lose aseity, then we lose God. If God is dependent on parts and people, then he's no different from the gods of Greek myth. He becomes another superhuman in the pantheon of deities. He fails to be the I AM. His name becomes meaningless.

God is his attributes

What is the implication of simplicity? The implication is that God doesn't have multiple attributes. This might be one of the lightbulb moments for you. It could be a shock. Perhaps you'll be tempted to resist it. I remember the first time I heard someone say this. It didn't sit right with me at all. But if God isn't made up of parts, then he can't have multiple attributes. Have a listen to the words of Irenaeus,

He (God) is a simple, uncompounded Being, without diverse members, and altogether like, and equal to himself, since he is wholly understanding, and wholly spirit, and wholly thought, and wholly intelligence, and wholly reason, and wholly hearing, and wholly seeing, and wholly light, and the whole source of all that is good.[7]

Mark Jones observes,

God is not simply good, but goodness itself. God is not merely powerful but rather omnipotence itself. More than that, when we speak of his attributes, we must keep in mind that because his essence remains undivided, his goodness is his power. Or God's love is his power is his eternity is his immutability is his omniscience is his goodness, and so forth.[8]

---

[7] Irenaeus, *Against Heresies* 2.13.3, in *the Ante-Nicene Fathers,* vol. 1, *The Apostolic Fathers: Justin Martyr, Irenaeus* (New York: Charles Scribner's Sons, 1903), 374.
[8] Mark Jones, *God is: a devotional guide to the attributes of God* (Illinois: Crossway, 2017), 31-32.

What does all of this mean? It means that God is eternally, unchangeably, infinitely, blessedly, powerfully, lovingly, mercifully good. If you're still struggling to picture it, imagine a prism for a moment. A prism is a triangular glass object which shows a spectrum of colours. From one side we observe all kinds of beautiful colours. We see yellows, reds, greens and blues. But from the other side, we realise that there's only one white light. So while it appears that there are many different colours, there is only one light. To change the analogy, think of the stain-glassed windows in Anglican churches. From the inside the stain-glassed windows create vibrant and colourful rays of light. And yet when we walk outside, we notice it's just the one light of the sun. God's attributes are a little like that. To us, it appears that God has multiple different attributes like love, goodness, mercy, justice, power and holiness. But to God, he is his attributes. They are all one in God.

Truth to anchor the soul

Why do we need to know this? How does it help? First, the simplicity of God is important because it's true. But second, the simplicity of God anchors the soul and brings immense comfort. Mark Jones helps us to grasp this by reflecting on Romans 8:28. Have a listen to this promise of God's word.

"And we know that for those who love God all things work together for good, for those who are called according to his purpose."

It's safe to say that this is one of the most well-loved and well-known promises in the entire Bible. For millennia, the saints have anchored their weary and fearful hearts on its truth. Here's how simplicity ties into it. Because God is goodness, he is good to make this promise to us. It's not something he can turn on and off. God is his goodness. But God's goodness is also his almighty power and so he is powerfully good to deliver on it. If that's all we had, it would be good news indeed. But it gets better! God is wisdom and knowledge and so he is powerfully good and powerfully wise to bring it about. And if we add that God is unchangeable in his essence, then we can trust that God will assuredly bring this promise to bear because he is immutably good, powerful, wise, knowledgeable and so on. Everything that God does, he does with all of these attributes. If God's attributes were divided, then we would never know if could was willing or able to come through on his promises. If goodness wasn't something that God had, then perhaps tomorrow he will decide to be the opposite. If wisdom is something God has, then he might be able to lose it. But if God is his attributes, then God's people can rest their souls on his perfect character.

The cross of Calvary

One of the central claims of the Bible is that at the cross of Christ we see all the attributes of God in their perfect glory. Thomas Boston once said,

> In the work of redemption, all God's perfections and excellencies shine forth in their greatest glory.

The cross of Calvary is central to God's plan to redeem a people for himself. Everything in the Old Testament is looking forward to that moment. In the New Testament Jesus comes to die on the cross. The cross is the place where atonement was made. It's the only way for rebel sinners to be made right with holy God. And it's also the place where God reveals his attributes. At the cross we find God's goodness, power, love, wisdom, holiness, justice, and righteousness. We meet a God who is all of these things all at once. God could not sweep sin under the rug and pretend it never happened. Nor would God abandon the whole human race to a lost eternity. Because God is his attributes, he made a way to satisfy his justice and save his people out of sheer grace. This is the beauty of God. This is the love of God. This is why simplicity is such good news.

4

IMMUTABLE

Change pervades our lives. *We blossom and flourish as leaves on the tree, and wither and perish.* We could say that one of the things that remains unchanged is the fact that we are subject to change. We change for better, and we change for worse. We change as we grow older, and we change in our personality. We change in our taste of music, and we change in our taste for food. We change in our attitudes, and we change in our understanding. Joseph Stalin was once a young man training for the ministry. He ended up becoming one of the greatest villains in the 20th century. The Apostle Paul used to be a terrorist in the early church as he would find God's people and imprison them. He was even there as Stephen was stoned to death. He ended up being one of the greatest missionaries the world has ever seen. He changed from persecutor to gospel proclaimer. None of us would doubt that we are subject to the tick tock of time. All of us change as time moves on. Sometimes for better (Paul) and sometimes for worse (Stalin). And until fairly recently, no one would deny that God remains untouched by time. God is immutable, that is, he is unchanging. But recent scholars have tried to argue that all things are in a process of change, and since God is a thing in existence, then he must be subject to change as well. This, however, is wrong.

God is immutable

The Bible teaches that God is unchanging in his being. God is the absolute bedrock upon which everything stands and he's the only solid hope for his people. The 1689 confession of faith states that God is unchangeable. The Westminster shorter catechism says this,

God is eternal and unchangeable in his being, wisdom, power, holiness, justice, goodness and truth.

As we continue to study the doctrine of God, we need to remember that this is an exercise of faith. We walk by faith, not by sight. If we try to map our experience onto God, then we would probably deny God's immutability. When we engage with creation, we recognise that everything is subject to change, and so we naturally want to map our experience onto God. But if we seek to reason from the mutable creation to the immortal, invisible God, then we'll run into error. Do you remember the illustration I gave of the Jenga tower? If we remove one piece of doctrine, then the others come crashing down too. This is true here. We need to go back to God's incomprehensibility because there is a vast chasm between Creator and creature. We don't have the option to go from creation to Creator, and that's because God is in a different category to us. This means that we can't try and figure God out by drawing implications from the natural world. The mutability of the creation doesn't imply the mutability of the Creator.

Rather than taking a punt at what God is like from the natural world, we will begin by jumping in a time machine and heading back to the days of Malachi. In Malachi's era, the people of God are enduring God's just judgements because the covenant lies in tatters. The nation of Israel is judged because of their stingy and corrupt offerings. It all started so well, and it's all ended so badly. And what stands out in the book of Malachi is the contrast between God and his sinful people. While Israel slides further and further into idolatry and unfaithfulness, God remains steadfast and immovable. Israel deserves to face God's swift execution. But God says something remarkable, "For I the LORD do not change, therefore you, O children of Jacob are not consumed" (Malachi 3:6). The order of this sentence is key. The 'therefore' is the hinge in Malachi's argument. The reason that God's people endure and are not destroyed is because of God's unchanging nature. It is because God is unchanging in his character that he is unchanging in how he operates with the nation of Israel. God doesn't change in who he is, therefore, he doesn't change in what he does. The faithfulness of God stems back to his covenant promises to Abraham, Isaac, and Jacob. God made a covenant commitment that he'd remain faithful to Abraham and his offspring. And the whole Bible is the unfolding of God's covenant commitment to his rebellious and sinful people.

The ever-changing God?

But what would happen if God were subject to change? What then? Does it even matter? Put simply, if God could change then he would cease to be God. Why is that? Because you can only change for better, worse or addition. Let's imagine that God changed by becoming more loving and merciful. If God changed by becoming more loving and more merciful, then we would have to admit that he was less than perfect before. But what if God became less merciful and loving? Then we would have to conclude that God was perfect in the past, but he has ceased to be perfect. But what about if God simply added something that he didn't have? If God added something to himself then he's not the One undivided Being. To add something assumes that God has parts and since God has no parts, he cannot add to himself. In each case, a changeable God would be a God that ceases to be eternally perfect. Any change in God would make God go from better to worse, or from worse to better. And since that's not possible we conclude that immutability is essential to God's identity.

Where immutability fits in

As we gathered from the chapter on God's simplicity, God doesn't have separate attributes as though he is divided, because what God has,

God is. In other words, God is his attributes. Yet while this is the case, because of accommodation, we need to distinguish between the attributes in order to grow in our understanding of who God is. One of the ways we do that is to figure out how each attribute hangs together. Immutability doesn't just hang by itself, but it's indispensable for every other attribute that God has. Stephen Charnock once wrote, "Immutability is a glory belonging to all the attributes of God because it's the centre where they all unite."[9] First, God is unchanging because he is the God of aseity. People change because they are dependent on other things to make them who they are. If God was subject to change, then we would need something else to be who he is. This would defy God's aseity and imply that he is a dependent being. Second, God is unchanging because he is a simple being. If God changed, then we would have to infer that God was made up of parts.

[9] Stephen Charnock, *The Existence and Attributes of God.* 2 vols. In one. 1853. Reprint, Grand Rapids, MI: Baker, 1996

Change in God would mean separating or adding something to him, which would mean that he is no longer the One, undivided Essence. Third, God is unchanging because he is all-powerful. If God could change in his power, then there was a time when God was limited in what he could do. But Isaiah says that God's power is unchanging because he is the Everlasting One who doesn't grow faint or weary (Isaiah 40:28). Fourth, God is unchanging because he's all-knowing and all-wise. No one has ever helped God out, instructed him, taught him knowledge, or increased his insight, because there is no searching of his understanding (Isaiah 40:13-14, 28). If God could change in what he knows, then there would have been a time when God didn't know all things, which leads to flawed or inaccurate knowledge. If God learned something today that he didn't know yesterday, then we'd have no reason to trust that his knowledge tomorrow will be accurate. Maybe God will get it wrong? If that's the case, then the God of the Bible is a scary God to trust in.

Finally, because God is unchanging, he is love. This is one of the greatest causes of Christian assurance and hope. What would happen if God were to change in his love? What assurance would we have in his election of us? If God changed in his love, then the doctrine of justification by faith alone would be the first thing to go. The reason that we can have hope when we get out of bed in the morning is because our God is unchanging in his love towards us. The Psalmist sings, "Give thanks to the LORD for he is good, his steadfast love endures forever." (Psalm 136:1). God is stubborn in his covenant commitment, and his love will never fail. As sinners saved by grace, we waver in our love for God. It's a dangerous game clipping our assurance onto our own spiritual pulse. There's barely a drop of assurance to be found in looking within. Assurance of salvation comes when we look at Christ and God's unchanging character. It's true that we don't often experience the same level of God's love. Sometimes the feeling wavers, and that's sometimes because of our own sin. Thankfully, our salvation isn't contingent on our feelings. My salvation rests in a *love that will not let me go.*

But what about *nikham*?

At this point, let me anticipate some objections. "But what a minute" – you might be saying – "Doesn't the Bible tell us that God changes his mind? Isn't that change in God"? Great question! If you have a Bible handy, head over to Genesis 6. You may know the chapter well. To say that things are bad at this point is an obvious under-statement. The fifth verse is a damning diagnosis of the human condition, "the wickedness of man was great in the earth, and every intention of the thoughts of his heart was only evil continually." It doesn't get much worse than this. God made humanity to know him and to spread his glory across the face of the earth through multiplication, but instead we decided to live for our own glory and follow the wicked desires of our hearts. And here's the thing I want us to notice. After the corruption of humanity hits new heights, God declares that he regrets (*nikham*) ever making us (v. 6). Surely this suggests a change of mind on a face-value reading? Now take a trip forward to the book of 1 Samuel 15. God gives Saul a crystal clear command, "Go and wipe out the Amalekites. Smash them into oblivion. Oh... and wipe out all the animals too." Saul gets to work, keeps the king alive, and saves the goodies for himself. Then in verse 35 we read, "And the LORD regretted that he made Saul king over Israel." Same pattern. Same problem. Same word. Same result. God's command is rejected, and God changes his mind. What can we say to these things? We need to remember that the Bible is a book of God's word to us. God is incomprehensible and so he speaks earthy, human words. God speaks with analogy to help us understand something of his character. So when it says that God has hands, eyes, feet, and wings, we know instinctively that God doesn't have these things. The same is true for these so called "problem" passages. God isn't repenting or changing his mind as we would imagine it. Instead, God is drawing us into the narrative in a way we can understand. When God says that he regrets making humanity, it's to make us sit back and go, "Wow!!!! It's gotten that bad!?" Think of the example with Moses on Mount Sinai. When God tells Moses that he'll destroy the Israelites – and then doesn't – it's not because God had changed his mind. God is inviting Moses into the conversation and bringing Moses in to mediate on behalf of the nation, and it's this pleading that achieves God's purposes from eternity. Throughout these episodes, God does what he was always going to do. Consider the episode with Jonah and the Ninevites. God sends a warning that he's going to destroy the people of Nineveh, and then seemingly changes his mind and delivers Nineveh from disaster! This is what makes Jonah so upset and frustrated. And yet Jonah's words spell out for us that God's plan was always to extend his mercy: "O LORD... I knew that you are gracious and merciful, slow to anger and abounding in steadfast love and relenting from disaster." (Jonah 4:2). Jonah knew that mercy was God's plan all along. God sent Jonah to threaten Nineveh with judgement, and then used that threat as a means to turn them from their sin. From our perspective, it looked like God was promising destruction and then changed his mind. But what God was doing was using the warning to cause repentance. God didn't change his mind but fulfilled what he immutably willed from eternity past.

What about Jesus?

A final objection would be the person of Jesus Christ. Doesn't the incarnation reveal a change in God? God was without a body from eternity past. But now he has a body because he took on flesh 2000 years ago. Didn't Jesus empty himself of his deity? Doesn't this prove that God has changed? These are good questions, but they fail to recognise the distinction between the two natures of Christ. When God took on flesh, the divine nature did not merge with a human nature. While the two natures hold together in the person of Christ, they are distinct. The divine nature didn't take on any properties of the human nature, and vice versa. Jesus needs to be truly God and truly man for us and for our salvation. Any change in either is detrimental for salvation and for the God-head. For this reason God did not change when Christ took on flesh. And yes, we affirm that Jesus emptied himself in the incarnation (Philippians 2:7), but that doesn't mean that he emptied himself of his divinity. The passage tells us that Jesus emptied himself by addition, not subtraction. He emptied himself by taking the form of a servant, being born in the likeness of men, and by being found in human form (vv. 7-8). There was no change in God's Being when the Son took on flesh.

Why we need immutability

I remember teaching through the immutability of God during a prayer meeting. At the end of the night, a young man approached me. I knew that he'd been having a hard time at work and was feeling the pressure. I was surprised to even see him at the prayer meeting. What caught me off guard was when he said, "Work has been incredibly stressful. I almost didn't make it this evening. And yet what I needed more than ever was to be lifted from the daily grind of ordinary life to the God who sits unchanged in the heavens. What a joy and comfort to know that the One who holds me is unchanging in his love and power." I wonder if that strikes you as a bit odd? I hope by now that you can see how practical and life giving a tour of the attributes of God can be for the soul. We instinctively think that what we need more than ever is to read a 5-step book on how to please God at work and how to use our retirement for the glory of God. All those things have a place.

But what we need more than anything is to know the God who loves us and holds us. Immutability is good news because it means God is steadfast in his covenant love for sinners. It means that I know with absolute certainty that his love for me won't wax and wane depending on my performance. He is my Rock, my Anchor, the captain of my salvation. And that salvation is as unchanging as Christ himself, the one who is the same yesterday, today and forever (Heb. 13:8).

5

IMPASSIBLE

Many people think of God as a deeply needy and emotional being, sitting in the heavens, always moments from striking us down in his anger. This image comes across in cinema across the world. You might think of the Hollywood version of the Exodus movie starring Gerard Butler. God appears as a trigger-happy child, ready to snap at any given moment. But is this the God of the Bible? Does that best reveal what God is like? As we consider the impassibility of God, we will discover that the answer is no. I have a sneaking suspicion that this is one of the most rejected (or neglected) aspects of the doctrine of God. It's counterintuitive and if I'm being honest... it took a long time to sit right with me.

The reason why we must uphold the doctrine of God's impassibility is because it is the logical implication of aseity and immutability. It's a necessary doctrine and yet it's foreign and neglected because of the way our culture has influenced our thinking about God, and human emotions. And so what is it? Impassibility is that God doesn't suffer, nor is he suspectable to emotional fluctuation. The 1689 confession of faith says,

God has no body, parts or *passions.*

Do you remember our time with the Greek gods? Let's head back to them for a moment because they're the best example of what we're trying *not* to say about the One true God of scripture. Take Zeus for example. Marvel's recent movie on Thor did a really good job of portraying Zeus' fluctuating character. One of the things that's hilarious about Zeus is that his emotional makeup is constantly changing. One moment he strolls about like a proud peacock parading his power, and the next he wallows in defeat and agony. He's a human with big superpowers, which means we can never trust him. He might be on your side on Monday, but come Thursday we'll never know if he's going to fly off the handle or not. Zeus (and all the Greek gods for that matter) are unable to control their emotions. But the God we worship is unlike the gods of pagan mythology. Michael Horton says,

"If God was changed by what we do, then we'd have no confidence that he, like Zeus, might not as easily destroy us in a fit of rage as weep helplessly over our condition."[10]

---

[10] Michael Horton, *Pilgrim Theology*, (Grand Rapids, MI: Zondervan 2011), 80

The God of the Bible is in complete control of who he is and what he does. God is never divided into different emotional states. He never gets overcome by sudden and unexpected mood changes. He's never anxious, lonely or compulsive.

God can't suffer

If God were passible, then he would experience inner human-like feelings which would bring comfort or discomfort. For example, if I do something sinful like taking advantage of someone else, then God's emotional gauge would fly to the miffed and angry side. If I did something good like driving an elderly member to the hospital, then God's emotional gauge moves to the happy side, which means he can enjoy himself again. Notice that in both cases God is dependent on me for his own emotional security. It's hard to see how God would be independent from creation. It's also hard to see how God wouldn't become the ultimate beneficiary of the new creation. If God suffers every time someone transgresses his law, then God would be undergoing the most pain and anguish of any being in the cosmos since all of humanity continues to sin against him. This suggests that heaven would then be the greatest relief for God (and that can't be right, surely!?)

For God to be impassable means that he doesn't undergo fluctuating emotions in a way that would cause him to suffer loss. It's worth taking out the pen and highlighting the word 'loss'. To say that God is impassable is to shield God from loss, which is why impassibility hinges on immutability. If God's nature cannot change, then it follows that he can't undergo emotional change. As we've already noted, if God was made to suffer by human sin, then he would be in a perpetually crippled state by the affairs of the world. Since God is independent from his creation, he can't be acted upon by the decisions that we make. This is what makes God different from his creation. Let me give an example. Imagine that you've decided to take a family trip to the beach for the day. It's summer, the kids are off school, and it's a gorgeous day. What would happen if after parking your car, someone rushed over and threw a brick into your window while the children are sitting in the back? I can tell you what would happen to me... I would begin to feel a rush of blood to the head as my heart begins to pump anger through my veins. And so notice what has happened. My emotional state is tethered to the actions of this individual. I was happy before he came along, and now I'm angry and frustrated. I am dependent on him for my own emotional welfare. This is where God is not like us. It can't be the case that God is dependent on me for his own emotional wellbeing. Whatever it means for God to get angry at sin, it can't mean what I've just described. Because the next question would be, "But doesn't the Bible say that God responds to sin with his anger?" I could reach into any place in the Bible and pull out multiple examples that show God responding to sinners with his wrath and anger. Doesn't that disprove impassibility? And doesn't God show love and mercy to his people?

What we need to recognise is that impassibility isn't affirming anything in the positive sense, it's simply a denial of the negative. This is how a lot of God's attributes work. Immutability is denying change in God; Aseity is denying dependency on God; Simplicity is denying parts in God; Infinity is denying finiteness in God. In each case, the attribute isn't telling us what God is like, but what he is not like. And so it's no surprise that impassibility works in the same way. Impassibility does not teach that God doesn't have love, and compassion, and it doesn't teach that the justice of God doesn't make him angry about sin. Impassibility teaches that God's love and justice are not true of God as a result of human behaviour. No living person can cause these virtues to exist in God, which means that impassibility protects God's attributes. It means that God's attributes don't fluctuate or change because of human activity. And it doesn't make God static. Rather, God is so alive, full and complete that he cannot become more loving and just than he already is.

Why we want an impassable God

Impassibility has found itself on hard times in recent years because the Western world has become focussed and obsessed with emotions and empathy. Joel Beeke writes,

Pop culture has elevated emotional sympathy to be a primary virtue. Therefore, when we consider what scripture teaches about God's affections, we need to be aware that strong cultural winds are pushing us towards the doctrine of a God who suffers with the suffering.[11]

---

[11] Joel Beeke, *Reformed Systematic Theology.* Vol 1. (Illinois: Crossway, 2019), 833.

I think Joel Beeke is onto something here. It seems that every song, movie and story is pulling us along on the tide of emotionalism and sympathy. If the chief virtue in our own age is to be sympathetic to others, then God must be the most sympathetic of all, and suffer for all. But I'm not really sure that's what we actually want. There are some occasions where I need to visit my doctor concerning the acid reflux that I suffer with. What do I want from the doctor as I pay him a visit? Do I want him to lie on the bed next to me in the attempt to force acid to run into his own oesophagus, that way he can tell me that he suffers alongside me? Or do I want a healthy doctor who's able to treat me and help me? I don't really care if the doctor can relate to me because that's not why I visited. I want to make sure that the doctor is in the right state to fix me. And the same is true for God. What I want is for God to come, not to share in my pain, but to set me free from it in the gospel. I want an unchanging God making irrevocable promises that he has done something decisively to rid the world of sin, misery and death. I want a God who screams, "it is finished" on the cross, which is exactly what we have in the person and work of Christ. A God who comes and suffers with me is of no use to me when what I need more than ever is a proclamation that sickness, death and hell have been defeated. This is precisely the God we receive in Christ.

Two common objections

As we bring this chapter to a close, it's worth briefly dealing with two common objections. Doesn't the Bible use emotional language when it refers to God? In Hosea, God declares that his heart recoils within him, and his compassion grows warm and tender (Hosea 11:8). Isn't that a good example of a God who has passions? And throughout the Bible, God declares that he has a holy hatred of sin? Shouldn't we assume that God is emotionally changing? These are fair and good questions. The

Bible definitely uses emotional language when referring to God, and it's here that we need to remember that God has accommodated himself to us by using human language so we can understand something of who he is. In other words, we need to read these passages analogically, not univocally. That doesn't mean we don't take them seriously. When it says that God loves us and delights in us, we need to take God at his word and rejoice in the truth of it. As God's people we rejoice to know that God's love is unchanging, powerful and complete towards us. Remember that impassibility means we cannot change or alter that. The same is true for God's response to sin. When it says that God hates sin, we need to take that seriously and recognise that God is in a composed state of hatred towards it.

The other objection I often hear is, "What about Jesus? Jesus is God... and didn't he suffer and have emotions?" I don't think anyone wants to deny that Jesus suffered and had emotions. The key with Jesus is to remember that he is one person with two natures. The assumption behind the question is that Jesus must suffer in his divine nature as well as in his human nature. The mistake is to merge the two natures together. While Jesus suffered on the cross as our human representative, he didn't suffer in his divine nature because the divine nature is impassable.

6

GOD REVEALED IN CHRIST

In this final chapter we will briefly consider John Calvin's musings that God is fully and finally revealed in Jesus Christ. The God who is incomprehensible to sinners, dwells in unapproachable light, that no one has seen or can see, has taken on flesh to dwell with us (John.

1:14). And God the Son did this without ceasing to God. Without ceasing to be what he already was, he became what he always was not. Jesus Christ, the Son of God is the ultimate and final means of God's revelation. John Calvin once said that since Christ has shone upon us, while before we only had a dim light, now we have the perfect radiance of divine truth. In the incarnation, all the other modes reach their highest fulfilment.

During the final discourse that Jesus had with his disciples, he revealed that he was the only way to the Father (John 14:6). Outside of Jesus and his finished work there is no reconciliation with God and no means to come to know God. Yet in the passage, we find that Jesus isn't just the way to God, but in him the Father is fully and finally revealed. If we want to know the Father, we must gaze at the glory of Christ. Jesus said, "Do you not believe that I am in the Father and the Father is in me? The words that I say to you I do not speak on my own authority, but the Father who dwells in me does his works" (v. 10).

The disciples have failed to recognise that knowing Jesus they know the Father. Their eyes will soon be opened as Jesus declares, "From now on you know him and have seen him" (v. 7). What is Jesus referring to? Jesus is referring to his brooding death, where he will offer up his life as a substitutionary sacrifice for his people, and this will declare to them the kind of God they serve.

Although the disciples will soon realise that Jesus is the full and final revelation of God the Father, there will still be a delay. We know this to be true because of Philip's response, "show us the Father" (v. 8). Rebuking Philip Jesus declares that he and the Father are one. Thus Jesus identifies himself with the Father, while also distinguishing himself from the Father. This means that the Father and the Son are identical in essence, but differ in Personhood.

The Father and the Son share the same divine essence and therefore they're identical in their attributes. John Calvin comments that in the Lord Jesus, "God has fully revealed himself, so far as God's infinite goodness, wisdom and power are clearly manifested in him." If we want to know God, then we must look to Jesus, for it is only Jesus who is the image of the invisible God and the one who makes him known (John. 1:18).

Printed in Great Britain
by Amazon

37201999R00046